I0447428

Warden Stories

GERALD BATTLE

outskirtspress
DENVER, COLORADO

The opinions expressed in this manuscript are solely the opinions of the author and do not represent the opinions or thoughts of the publisher. The author has represented and warranted full ownership and/or legal right to publish all the materials in this book.

Game Warden Stories
All Rights Reserved.
Copyright © 2015 Gerald Battle
v2.0

Cover Image by Gerald Battle

This book may not be reproduced, transmitted, or stored in whole or in part by any means, including graphic, electronic, or mechanical without the express written consent of the publisher except in the case of brief quotations embodied in critical articles and reviews.

Outskirts Press, Inc.
http://www.outskirtspress.com

ISBN: 978-1-4787-3982-1

Outskirts Press and the "OP" logo are trademarks belonging to Outskirts Press, Inc.

PRINTED IN THE UNITED STATES OF AMERICA

Contents

Preface

Game warden stories can be some of the most captivating tales known. They rank as challenges to credibility with some of those told by fishermen, a closely related bunch of characters. Whether these which follow rank in that category or not is for you to accept or reject, but they are true nevertheless. The assault on credibility is what contributes to their charm.

Game wardens, conservation officers, fish cops, forest fuzz, or whatever kind of name is contrived for those who try to make sure the natural resources are not depleted and which bounty is shared equally use the skills and acumen of the most competent detectives in order to effectively complete their mission. The best of them would equal the best of a big-city police department despite the often derogatory view of their endeavor. Evidence is usually gathered from the field, from the wild in addition to other normal sources.

Finding a needle in a haystack is moderately easy compared to finding a shell casing in 60 acres of woods. Matching tire tracks to a vehicle that might be 10 or more miles away was a challenge that might require the interview of a myriad of intelligence sources, some of which would have doubtful memory or veracity. We called these sources "cooperators." Some were natural- resource zealots who were extremely interested in protecting those resources. Some had only their self-interest at heart, such as a farmer who was tired of deer poachers tearing up his grain field with their cars. Others were interested in deflecting the officer's interest elsewhere, such as one who would complain about poachers several miles away when the officer got too close to their own poaching grounds. All this had to be sorted out by the officer in order to best utilize his own meager resources.

But among all this difficulty there were always humorous concoctions of the human mind when confronted with the reality that they were "caught." Sometimes the most unbelievable stories are contrived before being arrested. Some even continue afterwards despite the facts. Some unbelievable ones are even true and the suspect is released. Again, the officer is required to sort out what is fact, what appears to be intentional, what an innocent mistake.

Every officer has many tales to tell. These are some of mine.

The Job

The function of a Conservation Officer in the "old days" 35 or more years ago in Michigan, as it also may have been elsewhere, was certainly what could be called multi-faceted. We were far more than a simple "game warden." During any day, one might be called on to do many unexpected tasks in addition to the many that were planned. The nature of any law enforcement work obviously is to deal with the unexpected, but in addition there were many duties that mirrored many other occupations, and others that might be called administrative. We were assigned a specific area--usually a county, sometimes a portion of one. In that assigned area we were the whole Conservation Department to the public, a department that included experts in biology, fisheries, forestry, land and mineral management, and certainly public information, and these experts usually weren't available at the scene. You were the only one "on the firing line." When I was first assigned I remember a supervisor stating, "You are hired for a 40-hour week, but if you work only 40 hours you aren't doing your job." There were some sixteen-, even eighteen-hour days, but it averaged out to ten or eleven. But were those ten hours enjoyable and rewarding? For the most part, yes, or there would be few officers that stayed the course. Were there harrowing or boring times? That too, but that's what furnished the spice that kept it interesting.

Later on, officers were supposedly limited to forty hours a week, but what happens when you plan your day and an unexpected emergency or call to the other end of the county comes up? Either you try to make adjustments on a following day or you work "off the books." In your assigned area there was no second shift to take over. In our district each officer spent from 2040 to 2655 hours in one year, where a normal 40 hour week would amount to about 1960 hours per year. During that same year the officers in our district drove from 16,288 to 23,191 miles, all within their assigned areas.

In those days we drove our family car on duty, which of course for the most part deleted "family." By the time we loaded our patrol equipment into the car, some of the family might be left out. The miles we drove were not on an easy interstate. One of the prime considerations in buying a new car--which necessarily happened every two or three years—was: "How much ground clearance does it have?" a critical consideration on trail roads. One officer summarizing the concern for a new car's condition said that on receiving a new car you should immediately drive it at 60 miles per hour down the brushiest, ruttiest trail in your area. After that you didn't need to worry about its appearance any more.

The need for as much road clearance as possible was especially necessary in winter. Many times when patrolling a trail road if you weren't careful you'd get the feeling that the car was rising, much like an airplane just lifting off. Then you didn't move forward any more – you were stuck. The uninitiated driver would gun the engine, hoping to blast through, but usually all it did was get you stuck more severely with spinning wheels, which never did the transmission any good. So the usual routine--for me at least--was: get out the jack, jack up the car, take the shovel and shovel out as much snow under the car as you could, let the jack down, put it and the shovel away, then move cautiously forward again; forward because it was usually a long way to back up to clearer roadway. Then when you felt the take-off feeling again you got out the jack, got out the shovel, etc., as many times as it took to get through. But you were in the open air, the snow was pretty, and it was good exercise. Yeah, right. After a few of these you became more selective on routing.

Since you worked from home, the job entailed planning your day to be the best use of your time, with law enforcement obviously the prime concern. To put your time and efforts in the right place at the right time we used intelligence sources, called "cooperators." As already mentioned, the worth of this information varied. A little "grain of salt" and good judgment was necessary. Although law enforcement was our primary concern, other necessary duties presented themselves. Sometimes you had to be a road maintenance worker after driving a half-mile or so down a twisty trail road to encounter a washout with no room to turn around. Sometimes you had to be a diplomat, such as when encountering a drunken group of hunters, one or more of whom had violated the law. Sometimes you were a tourist guide assisting lost vacationers. Newly assigned to my county, even I got lost a few times. I could commiserate with people in a parked car scratching their heads with map unfolded and confused looks on their faces. Always you had to be on good terms with news media, feeding them good stories, even helping them write them occasionally. Often you were called on to be a presenter of information before groups, many times as a teacher or instructor. A very large part of our time was spent in public information. Checking on forest cuttings and mineral extractions on state land was often in the picture, which sometimes entailed quasi-engineering duties. In those days butchering was called for as you gutted out freshly highway-killed deer for school hot-lunch programs. At that time there was not so much concern about food quality. If it was a fresh kill and not badly broken up it was foolish to waste the meat. On the other side of that picture we were called on to be undertakers in burying too-badly-smashed or too-long-dead deer. This rather distasteful duty took up a very large part of our time and of course little of it was part of the day's plan, even on a day off. In those days we did this chore so that no one could have possession of a freshly killed deer out of season and claim they found it on the highway. Did some people pick up deer and make that claim? Of course, but they ran the risk of an arrest if they were caught. For possession of a freshly killed deer out of season there was no defense.

One evening a group of men were traveling on the highway and a deer ran out in front of them and they hit it. It was dark. They got out to see what damage had been done to the car and the deer. Because it was dark, they could see that apparently there was no damage to the car. They looked around for the deer, but they couldn't find it, so they concluded that it wasn't hurt badly and ran off. They continued down the road and a little later the car started overheating and something started to smell really bad. They stopped, made a closer search to the front of the car and found that the grill had swallowed the deer like a fish swallows a bait. The deer had lodged against the radiator, damaging it, causing the car to overheat (and partially cooking the damaged deer). It took a trip to the shop not only to repair the car, but also to extricate the deer.

Not only did cars take a toll on the deer, but domestic dogs running loose chased them either for a short bit of sport or something to chew on. Checking on this type of complaint took a great deal of time, with little chance of a remedy unless you were lucky enough to get there in time and get in front of them where you *thought* they would cross a vantage point so you could chase them off or shoot them, which conservation officers had the power to do at that time. Many seemingly feeble domestic dogs were terrors when they saw or smelled a deer. This often resulted in the exhausted deer going to water to escape, often to drown. If so, and if it washed up in a populated area there were usually complaints necessitating a burial. Dealing with a waterlogged deer with a decease date long in the past wasn't a pleasant part of the job. About all you could do was drag it as far away from water as you could and try to bury it as deep as you could. Sometimes it was so long deceased that it would come apart in the dragging process. Not fun.

One time I received such a complaint from a lady when her dog got into the smelly remains of a beached deer. I went there and buried the deer. A day later I got another more furious call via my district headquarters about the same deer. I explained that I had already taken care of it, but was told to take care of it *again*. Upon investigating I found that her same snippy little dog had dug it up *again*. This time it took a 25-mile trip onto the beach with one of our four-wheel drive fire trucks to move the remains far away from her little darling.

Another time I was called to a town one evening, the complaint being that two dogs had maimed a deer right on the outskirts. Several men chased the dogs off twice, but they returned each time. When I arrived there a small crowd of men had congregated and they pointed out the dog to me, about 100 yards away. The deer, a three-year-old buck, was down and one dog was next to it. I got out my rifle to dispatch the dog. Instantly one of the men shined his flashlight on the sights of my rifle, I shot, and the dog died without even yelling, "Cripes, cripes" to awaken the neighbors. Upon going over there I found that the dogs had completely stripped the hide off the deer's back, its haunches had chunks of flesh torn from them so that the deer couldn't run, and the deer was still alive--and the dog was no larger than a terrier. Even a dog that small is a hazard to deer, especially fawns. On thinking the situation over later, I wondered how the man knew to light up my sights and how many times he might have done it in the past.

Sometimes a surgeon's duty was called for when it was necessary to probe a carcass for a bullet to be matched to a gun. Sometimes it was necessary to be a "political person" as you escorted and explained

KILLED BY DOGS — This is what two dogs can do to a deer. Conservation officer Gerald Battle picked up this pitiable looking animal shortly after it died at Cedar early Easter Sunday morning. The hide had been entirely stripped from its back and even off its tail. Ragged chunks of skin and fur hung from its sides. The dogs had torn chunks of flesh from its haunches so that the deer was unable to run. It floundered around near the highway about 100 yards from the Solon town hall.

Several Cedar men drove the dogs off twice but they returned and continued to harrass the struggling animal. In the meantime Battle was called by Adolph Novak. The deer, a three-year-old buck, was dead when Battle got to Cedar. He killed one of the dogs which was still hanging about near the scene.

Battle said there have been an increasing number of reports recently of dogs running deer.

situations to much higher government officials, some with whom you might have disagreements. *Always* you had to operate similar to a CIA operative, hiding your intentions and location from the public, even working in disguise at times. Always it was necessary to be as secretive as possible. Since you were the only law enforcement entity of your type in a given area, you were watched as much as you watched others. This is different from other law enforcement personnel who might operate out of a post or a headquarters. In their case, the threat for a violator of the law might come from any officer, not just one. A case might be worked on by many officers during its life; for a conservation officer assistance from other officers who had their own concerns and territories would come only when the situation was almost out of hand. If you were really conscientious, this meant *always* parking your car in the garage with the doors closed, closing all drapes in the house at night, and never answering the phone after dark. This meant that a family member, usually your wife, had to get on the phone at 2:00 a.m. to answer an innocuous question from someone four beers from sobriety, but who agreed with companions to check the location of the game warden before we go and "see if we can get us a deer."

I would often on my day off dress in uniform, go to town, pick up mail, get the car gassed up, talk to people, and in general just be seen, then go home, change into "civvies" and take care of family matters like anyone on their day off. If this included engaging in a family affair where I would be seen in public, it was done outside my assigned area.

One time I was coming home early in an evening from patrol and was carrying my gear into the house when a known violator stopped at the house with an innocuous question. As we talked I turned and put my "stuff" back in the car as if I were going out instead of coming in. I made several trips back and forth as we talked, and ended up confused myself. Was I going or coming? If he was as confused as I was, I had met my objective.

I would often make a show of patrolling one end of the county, then driving to the other end to *really* patrol. This gained me the reputation of "being everywhere," which was my goal.

Was it a tough, nerve-wracking job at times? Did you really have to be dedicated (along with your family members)? Yes, but of course the offset was that you were working outdoors, the job was certainly not boring in the long run, and you were your own boss regarding working hours. And you never knew what interesting people or situations would come up next.

Where on Earth Am I?

Geography is a critical issue for a conservation officer. If s/he doesn't know the assigned area intimately, the job not only doesn't get done, but safety issues are involved, especially when a forest fire exists. Therefore an officer new to an area should be a very devoted geography student in learning not only the roads but also the topography of the area in the "back country." In a geographically diverse area you don't have to get far off the road to be in "back country." This learning effort is by no means a quick study. It's a constant learning process of a dynamic subject. Buildings are built, and roads and trails develop or deteriorate. I once came upon a house, probably in the $300K value range, and it befuddled me how a fire truck would be able to access it in an emergency via the two-track trail leading to it.

Upon being assigned to my area, the geography of which I was at least already somewhat acquainted with, I found many surprises. Even in a conventional township and section layout in relatively flat land where there may be straight roads every mile or so there are many challenges. In rugged country with hills and river, etc., where roads don't always point north and south or east and west, it can translate sometimes to "How in the hell did I end up here?" The politically polite term for lost is "discovers alternate destinations," and I own up to more than a few unexpected arrivals, even though I have a well-developed sense of direction.

After the learning process is well along, it becomes a teaching process. The most important "students" are the firefighters, who need to know the quickest way into a fire area, and if things go bad the quickest way back out away from the flames. Quite often in following trails into an area I would end up in a farmer's yard on the other end. This no doubt caused some consternation with the farmer wondering, "What's he doing on MY land?" but it was a necessary affront in an important learning process and added to the illusion that I "was everywhere."

Sometimes one of my cooperators would ask if he could go along with me on patrol. If it looked like a routine day (of course, you never knew for sure) I would allow it. Most of these folks were natives to the area; I was in the beginning an outsider. But I chuckled to myself when I often got the comment, "I never knew all this was here!"

One time a state trooper asked to accompany me, and I was glad for the company. We checked out an area in which he had an interest, and HE "discovered some alternate destinations" of which he hadn't been aware. A few years later he later was assigned to the governor's bodyguard unit, where such a phenomenon would certainly not be acceptable.

All in all, learning all about the geography and terrain of an area of 360 or so square miles and passing on that information to others was probably the most stimulating part of the job. There was always a discovery down the road.

Law Enforcement

The work of a conservation officer, except for the environment in which it is conducted, is much the same as any other law enforcement officers: a watchful waiting, observing what is going on, looking for oddities, anomalies, changes in the normal fabric of everyday living. Since these anomalies are usually few and far between, there's a lot of tedium in between, tedium that can dull the senses and spell the officer into inattention. It's often as depicted in war: months of monotony interspersed with a few minutes of sheer hell.

The watching is the first step. Very often when checking a fisherman or hunter you get the comment, "I've been fishing [or hunting] for [x number of years], and this is the first time I've ever been checked by an officer," to which the answer is usually, "Yes, but I'm sure you've been watched a few times."

When one of those moments occurs of watching an unusual break in what seems to be normal, the next step for a conservation officer is to get to the point of that anomaly quickly without being revealed or discovered. This is probably the most challenging part of the job. Observation is often employed from a somewhat distant location, or one that's concealed. After all, who is going to violate the law when s/he knows an officer is present? so distant locations and binoculars are usually employed, which gets interesting on a very cold day when it's hard to keep from shivering and the image is jumping around in the lens.

But then once something appears to be amiss the challenge and sometimes fun begins. How do you get from here to there quickly, quietly, and unobserved before evidence is lost while your own observation is stunted? If you are concealed from them, they are also concealed from you while you're moving, and who knows what's happening in the interim? So many times like these I wished I had a partner present who could help in this multi-tasking effort. But then when you look at the whole picture you're essentially inefficient during most of your unproductive patrols. Would not two officers patrolling together be even more wasteful?

During this phase of enforcement an officer becomes more like a predator attacking a quarry, almost more like a military attacker than a friendly public servant. I always felt a surge of pride if I could approach a hunter or a fisherman to a distance of a few feet before announcing my presence. You did it VERY carefully approaching a hunter with a gun. But when you could do this, "game wardens" were everywhere for that hunter or fisherman in the future: "You never know when one of them SOBs will turn up."

The next step was common to all law enforcement; finding out what's REALLY going on, sorting out fact from fiction, checking out stories and alibis--, another time when other law enforcement assistance is helpful when there are multiple suspects.

Enforcing the law in the winter was often tedious, boring, and non-productive. Hunting was mostly closed, so few people ventured out with a firearm – hard for them to explain, and with snow on the ground it's easy to be discovered. There were ice fishermen, of course, but by the time you walked out maybe a half mile on the ice they all knew you were coming and could change whatever illegal activities they were involved in. By the time you got out a few hundred yards in 15-degree weather with the wind at 10 knots or more you wondered whether it was worth it. But you were putting in an appearance, and you never knew what you might learn from the encounter.

But taking it all together, the challenge was stimulating to say the least and kept you sharp. There was a confined bay on a lake in my area where ice fishermen gathered every winter and where brown trout, which were out of season, hung out occasionally. There were cottages around it, not giving a great deal of cover for observation. So I dressed in plainclothes, grabbed some fishing gear, went down there, spudded a hole in the ice twenty yards or so from where they were and proceeded to pretend to fish. After a while one of them, a man whom I knew (and who knew me but didn't recognize me) yelled, "Hey Freddy, look what I caught!" Freddy, whom I also knew, went over there and investigated. I tried to see what it was without appearing to be curious, and saw him holding a brown trout, on which the season was closed.

I heard them talking, and Freddy said, "Oh, that's a trout. You're not supposed to take them this time of year."

"What? Sure you can. It's okay."

"No, I don't think so. John, you better put it back."

"No, that's a nice fish. I'm gonna take him."

Freddy, still shaking his head, went back to his own fishing.

A little later, John started packing up his gear and began walking toward shore. Seeing this, I gathered my stuff together and headed that way too, trying to get ahead with all haste to get there ahead of John, stash my stuff, then meet him at his car. Going fast while looking ordinary and in no hurry is an acquired skill that most officers get eventually. However, I did so, puffing a bit from the exertion, and said upon arriving, "Hi John, how was the fishing?"

"Oh, not so good. I only got a few little ones."

"How about the brown trout you got?"

His eyes just about popped out of his head; then he admitted taking it. When I saw him a few months later he said, "I could never figure out how you knew I had that trout, but I finally did. That other guy out on the ice there had a radio under his coat, and he called you in."

I never told him the truth: that it was me all along. That was one that worked out well, was relatively easy, was fun besides--and I'm sure cooled some future potential violations.

Will This Day Never End?

One of the most memorable days in my career started following attendance at a movie with my wife on the eve of Memorial Day. I had had complaints of people taking smallmouth bass with a spear in the bay of Lake Michigan near our home. After dropping off my wife at 11:30 p.m. I went down to the bay and watched a boat with underwater lights cruising back and forth. At approximately 2:00 a.m. they came to the landing where I lay hidden. There were three men in the boat. One took a gunny sack and walked toward town, about a quarter of a mile off. I was in a dilemma whether to follow him or to watch what the other two were doing, but since he already had a head start, I stayed put. Soon I announced myself and one man began doing something behind the stern of the boat. I hurried over there and found some smallmouth bass on a stringer, which were illegal to be taken. I also found a spear in the boat, which I took for evidence along with the fish.

I identified them and summoned them in to court and went home to bed at 3:30 a.m. At 9:30 a.m. I was back on duty, went to the south end of a nineteen-mile-long lake and started a boat patrol of fishermen there. There were many of them to check, so it was a slow patrol. At 12:30 p.m. I found a juvenile fishing in a closed area, so I took him to his parents, explained the situation, warned them, then continued my patrol. At 3:00 p.m. I checked a boat with three fishermen in it. One had taken a smallmouth bass out of season and another had no fishing license. I summoned them in to court and attempted to take their fishing poles as evidence, but they, partly inebriated, moved them to the far side of their boat out of my reach. I worked my way over there, and they shifted them back to the other side. We patrolled with very light round-bottomed boats and 5 horsepower motors in those days, and I could see that further effort on my part was going to result in at least one of us--probably me--in the lake, so I broke off, went to a town within our view and asked for assistance from the sheriff's department.

After a while a deputy showed and we began searching for them. They were not to be found on the lake in the immediate vicinity, but we found them in a nearby bar. By now more influence than a summons was apparently necessary, so we took them directly to court. One subject refused to post bond so we took him all the way back again across the county to jail. After I was returned to my boat by the deputy I continued my patrol and found a father without a license fishing with his two boys. Giving him a summons to court was the normal procedure, but do law enforcement officers ever get lazy? Well--while not admitting to "lazy," I was at least guilty of "wasted," since after a long day and having ten or more miles to my point of embarkation and in the interest of not embarrassing him completely before his kids, I gave him a stern lecture and went on to my landing place, loaded the boat, and ended my patrol after 16 hours of duty. It was a trying day over and above the span of time, but productive.

Routine

It was not always as frantic as this; often it was boring as you patrolled and observed activities in your area, which were sometimes scant. As mentioned, part of the job was to be completely aware of the topography, roads and trails in your assigned area. So if there wasn't much going on you were patrolling remote areas and making some interesting discoveries, such as abandoned farmhouses in the midst of grown-up woods, a few trysting places, sites of teenaged beer parties, and foundations of old trapper cabins. The unexpected was always possible, almost like being in a war zone, except that no one was shooting at you--well, almost no one, because officers have been targets. We wore sidearms and had strong enforcement powers because of this fact. As mentioned, one of our powers was to shoot and kill dogs running deer. However, a supervisor warned us, "You can do almost anything demeaning to a man and get by, but if you shoot his dog he'll be an enemy forever." It was wise advice.

One time I had a complaint about dogs running deer on a huge sand dune in the county and they were doing it quite regularly. I spent more patrol time in the area and soon heard the yapping of dogs on a trail. They were on the top of the dune about 100 feet above me, and I had to intercept them there. I ran up the dune, which is usually the traditional "two steps forward and one step back" as I struggled in the soft sand. By the time I got to the top, carrying binoculars, rifle and a map board, I was well behind them, and with my heart about to leap out of my chest couldn't have placed a shot anywhere near them even if I was on time.

I retreated down the dune, making that trip MUCH faster, got in the car, drove downtrail in time to get off a shot there, but missed, but at least scared them off the trail, which allowed me to identify the dogs. I had heard that there was a possibility that they were owned by our park manager of the park of which the dunes were a part. A bit later I went to his house and talked to him. He recognized the seriousness of the situation, not the least of which was the notoriety, but he said he didn't think so because his dogs were always tired and sleeping. Indeed they were! After runs of two or three miles across sand they were bushed! I identified them as the culprits and he sadly asked if I would shoot them. I told him that I couldn't shoot them like that; it wasn't in me, although I would have relished killing them on the trail. So, I think I kept a friend, but a very sorrowful one, as he himself had to deal with his errant canines.

Up the Stream, Up the Stream

One of my annual frantic periods was when the smelt ran out of Lake Michigan in the spring. The smelt is a forage fish, 7 to 12 inches long, much eaten by larger fish and eagerly by local people. They're said to taste like cucumbers, but I could never attest to that. They were good, but cucumbers? Nah. They ran up the streams in early spring at night, about the first hint that winter was breaking. It was legal to take them with dip nets and it was often a party occasion as "dippers" congregated along the streams. Most of our problems were nuisance complaints: trespass and late-night carousing, for which we weren't the primary enforcement agency. But we were there anyway--because, well, they were fishermen, and fishermen were our concern.

Usually when not annoyed the smelt would come into the streams in thousands, do their spawning, and leave. When smelt dippers were present and active it would be a cycle of dipping, followed by the fish running back downstream out of danger, then congregating again at the mouth to make a later sprint. During this interim the dippers would leave the stream for a while during which time a few (or more) beers would be consumed while someone carefully checked the stream with a flashlight to see if the fish had returned, then when they had, the dipping cycle would be repeated.

However, it was necessary that dippers have a fishing license, which was sometimes hard to enforce when you started checking licenses in a group of six or more fishermen in the dark of night when someone could slip away. Because of the nature of the situation we sometimes patrolled with sheriff's deputies who were more concerned with the nuisance problem and could be a second pair of eyes.

I had numerous complaints from a man who lived right on the banks of one of the streams. I tried to answer them as best I could, but had a whole county to watch over. I sympathized with him, as had our department, which had closed the stream to dipping, but I just couldn't camp there every night. However, one night I got lucky. After several groups had been warned off the stream, about 1:00 a.m. two people came walking up the shore and entered the creek, dipping. They were shortly joined by three more. I called them out in a loud voice to come up on the stream bank. It was one of the surprises of my career that they complied: no one tried to slip away in the darkness. I checked their licenses and stories, one of which was that they were staying at their cottage a few hundred yards down the beach; however, they couldn't come up with the name of the person they allegedly bought it from, a name I knew. That and a few other misrepresentations persuaded me that a simple warning was not appropriate. As I began to write them up, one of them began to get belligerent. At a time like this--early in the morning, dark, one officer, and five unfriendly perpetrators--it begins to test one's diplomacy. You don't want to rile them, but backing down is also not an option. We "discussed" the matter for quite some time, and it ended up with the most vociferous of them insisting on going before a judge right then instead of being summoned in for the next day. Since it was nearly 3:00 a.m. by now, I suggested it might not be a good idea, but he insisted. Upon getting the judge out of bed, the perpetrator began giving him a dose of what I had been getting for the past hour. Unfortunately for him it didn't help his case very much when it came time for the sentencing.

Another time I checked a lone smelt fisherman on a stream for a license and he had none. As I was writing him up I noticed a small brook trout caught in his net, a youngster who apparently had been swimming in the wrong company. I mentioned to the individual, "I think you want to let that brookie go back in the water before he dies, don't you?" He looked in his net, almost jumped out of his skin, answered apologetically, and quickly let the fish swim, anticipating another ticket which I would have forgiven under the circumstances.

People Are the Most Fun

One of the best features of my area was that it was populated with different ethnic groups, the members of which were often colorful. Upon noting that the smelt left the stream when disturbed, one of my "characters" noted, "I don't know why dey do dat, dese fish in the bucket don't tell no stories."

On another occasion during deer season an officer got complaints about, "No deer." He explained that there were plenty of tracks around, whereupon the complainant remarked, "Yah, but dose tracks make mighty t'in soup."

There was to be a wedding in the county in a family reputed to be heavy deer poachers. The rumor came to me that they were going to go out the night before to get a deer to share at the reception. My partner and I found a hiding place on a trail road across from their farm, so we parked the car there in the woods. After a while a car left the house, went into their back orchard and began shining a light around. Because of the terrain we couldn't see clearly, so we left the car to get a closer look. All of a sudden we had to duck in the brush as the car came toward us. Then it turned into the very trail road on which we were parked! We ran to overtake them and did so, just about the time they spotted our car. I caught up with the car just in time to almost catch parts of a shotgun that were being ditched out the window of the car. When I apprised them of this fact, they denied all knowledge of the gun even when I told them that it was legal by the time I saw it (it was legal in Michigan to have a gun in a game area if it was in a case or broken down). Still they denied ownership. However, one noisy individual stated that he had been to law school and we couldn't do anything to them "because we didn't comprehend them on a public highway." I didn't know what law school he went to, but it was obvious it was going to be hard for him to pass the bar exam.

Every place has people who would be called "characters." I was blessed in my area by having many of them: people who didn't feel that they had to be sophisticated, but who were just themselves and who were not afraid to express themselves frankly. We need more like them.

I'm reminded of an old-timer who worked a small sawmill with his brother. Their home was very small and humble and said to have only a dirt floor. Apparently he had run into enough trouble between alcohol and driving that he no longer had a driver's license. Not being dismayed by this (and not complaining) he just simply traveled about the county the best way he had available: by walking. Quite often I would find him ten or more miles from home, happily on his way, most always with a happy word or two. One time he admitted to not being able to hear very well, his comment being, "Too much sawdust in my ears, I guess."

Brothers Together

Despite many stories of national enforcement agencies being sometimes very jealous of their "turf," we worked well together on the most part at the local level. At the core was a *respect* for turf and being careful not to step into the other guy's cornfield without close coordination. Early in my career I answered a complaint of a deer hunter lost at night in a four-square-mile swamp. The call had gone first to the state police, who were on the scene and who turned the matter over to me, but I knew that the safety of the citizenry was the purview of the sheriff. So, while I was the action officer at the scene, I kept in close contact with the sheriff and let him do the directing. I went in along with a couple of other hunters and found the man. He was beginning to become frantic. He had on World War II leather bomber pants which were torn and shredded from barging around in the brush, but we brought him out. I think the action of asking for the sheriff's direction and giving him credit for the rescue paid off in our later relationship.

Our law enforcement resources were slim during that period, and co-operation was the key. Often I was the only enforcement unit of any kind on the road, so I was the eyes and ears for other agencies. While conservation officers in Michigan at that time were fully empowered peace officers and could apprehend for traffic and other violations, we kept our noses out of that field. At times, though, when witnessing a flagrant traffic violation I would stop the individual, get information, and turn it over to the state police or sheriff for their further action, if any, but I would end there.

One time there was a tragic drowning of a young boy on Lake Michigan. He had been fishing with his father, the boat overturned, and the father was rescued, but the boy was not. This was the concern of the sheriff, but at that time he had no boats--I did. So I found myself in company with a deputy sheriff searching for the boy's body. After a couple of days of fruitless searching we ended up with three agencies working together: Conservation, Sheriff and State Police divers.

At another time the sheriff had some suspects in jail for breaking and entering. The evidence indicated that they had also shot a deer out of season. So a state trooper, the sheriff and I were traveling across the county to their home in the trooper's police car when right in front of us a car pulled into an intersection without stopping. The trooper stopped him and approached the car. He spoke to the driver for a couple of minutes, then looked up to the sky and shrugged his shoulders. Upon his coming back to the patrol car, the sheriff asked him if he gave the man a ticket. The trooper in exasperation said, "I asked him what he was thinking., driving through a stop sign, and he said, 'I'm sorry, officer, I was praying.' How could I give him a ticket? But I warned him he'd better pray that he drive more safely in the future."

Sometimes it's not a good idea to call in other enforcement agencies. One dark night my patrol partner and I were watching a stream in the fall when brown trout were spawning. We had checked the creek just a few minutes before, and two nice-sized trout were in the stream just below us next to the road culvert.

Very soon a car came up, stopped at the culvert, a man got out, and the car went a few more yards and parked. As we watched, the man who had got out shot into the stream with a pistol right where we saw the fish. We gave chase, apprehended them, but found no pistol. We were in a cedar marsh and I had caught up with the shooter after he had gone into the marsh. We knew we had a case, we knew a gun was involved, and one of them had shot at a fish, but where was the gun in the marsh? One of the subjects was a part-time deputy sheriff who had on his Sam Brown belt over civilian clothes, and he claimed that he was on duty (which the sheriff denied) and they had been checking some property nearby for trespass. I needed the gun for evidence and needed help in searching for it. The sheriff's office was only three miles away, the state police post about eighteen. I radioed the post for assistance because of the sensitive nature of the situation. Although they said they would dispatch a couple of troopers, it would take an hour or more for them to get there since they were at the other end of the district, and they insisted that the sheriff was more available, but I didn't want to discuss that aspect on the radio. They contacted the sheriff. A deputy arrived shortly and I explained the situation and that I could understand if he didn't want to help. His answer was "Oh, (expletive deleted)," but he helped somewhat anyway. After about twenty minutes of search the pistol was found and I took it as evidence. It was a ticklish situation, but the sheriff and I, after a bit of haughtiness, were able to work together afterwards. I'm not sure whether the part-time deputy ever received any more assignments, but he was essentially suspended in the short term.

The subject who had done the shooting either thought that he had a good case for acquittal or didn't want the notoriety of a conviction, so he pled not guilty upon arraignment. The court trial was set up for a future date and he hired a local attorney, of which there were only about three in the county in those days, and whom I knew quite well, having had personal dealings with him. Excessive litigation was at that time unknown. Most people settled their differences by a low-grade altercation or mostly they just took differences as a fact of life and moved on. At the trial I was called to testify and the defense attorney, knowing he had a poor case and needing to gain points, upon my taking a seat at the witness chair, jumped up and stated vehemently, "Judge, this man brought a firearm into your court!"

The judge was somewhat nonplussed by this, as was I, and some in the jury gasped while others snickered, but he asked me, "Why the gun?" I replied that it was part of my uniform, and since I was in uniform, I was wearing it. Upon further objection by the attorney the judge said that perhaps I'd better hand it over to him anyway, upon which I unloaded it and passed it to him. The theatrics didn't work, however, because the jury found the defendant guilty.

This was one of only three not guilty pleas I received among hundreds of arrests during my time as a conservation officer. I didn't take many "iffy" cases. When I handed over a summons I had them solid and locked.

In our county, which was not at all overpopulated, a good officer learned to know and get along with as many people as possible. Knowing the defense attorney in this case was no problem for either of us. We did our jobs the best we could despite being on opposite sides. I even had to arrest the county treasurer at one time. He had done what many deer hunters did--shoot more deer than his legal limit so that others in his party would have their deer. When there is a drive on and the drivers are the "dogs" chasing the deer, those posted at the end of the drive usually did the shooting, then possession of the downed deer was parceled out. Unfortunately for the treasurer, however, his "capture" was witnessed by a gabby witness. He was no more in the wrong than most hunters, but wrong nevertheless, and I had to deal with it according to law.

Another Long Night

On another occasion I was scheduled to appear for a promotional examination the next day at 8:00 a.m. The evening before I received a complaint that nets had been set in the waters of a nearby bay. Besides netting smelt in streams with dip nets, it was also legal for people to procure a commercial license and set a gill net in certain allowable waters of Lake Michigan. A provision of the law required that these nets be identified with a marker buoy showing the license number of the fisherman using them. Upon investigation my patrol partner and I found two nets with no markers. Along with my partner, we watched the area from a hidden spot. We watched and we watched. At 1:30 a.m. the watching paid off as men went out from shore to retrieve one of the nets. On their return we arrested them and confiscated their net.

Realizing that our cover was now blown, we relaunched our boat and pulled the other net. Both had been in the water long enough to make a plentiful catch. It would be wasteful to let them rot, so we went 30 miles to the district office and garage where we could rack and clear the nets. On our way to headquarters we came upon a car parked in the middle of the highway. I got out and checked, and it was obvious they were three sheets to the wind. I checked the driver's license; he was from the same city we were going to. We were only two miles from it, and he was asking in a bleary voice where it was. It was obvious he was in no condition to drive. I asked the other three people in the car if they could drive, and all I got in return was silence from droopy-lidded people. I called the state police to see if they had a car in the area, which they did not, so I asked them for instructions. I was told to lodge the driver in the county jail. By now, almost 3:00 a.m. with a car full of smelly fish, I had few other alternatives than to abandon the other three people and haul the driver off to jail. We then proceeded to head-quarters, started clearing the nets, then I returned home at 5:30 a.m.

Up again, I tried to be bright-eyed for the exam at 8:00 a.m., but didn't really succeed very well. I was then back on duty at 11:00 a.m., assist-ing a state trooper for that traffic violation, then continued clearing nets of smelt and delivering them to the county farm. It was an inter-esting full night and day, but not one I would like to repeat.

The Biggest Challenge – and Victory

Toward the end of a deer season I received a complaint of a subject who had shot a deer illegally, dragged it out to the road, and stated, "I wish my brother would hurry up with the car." Toward the end of the season, many times hunters would get anxious and careless and shoot at anything, legal or not. I was given a name and a location, but that wouldn't support a conviction unless the informant would testify, and all I had was a recalcitrant voice on a phone. I had a possible violation that could vanish into thin air, my patrol partner and I hurried to the location in the hope that we could gather enough evidence.

Sure enough, we found an untagged dead doe that had been dragged to the edge of a road. Okay, now what? We had proof of a violation, but who did it? The informant had given me a name, but even that proved nothing. The informant could be someone with a grudge. We followed the drag marks back to where they began and found a pile of entrails, obviously where the deer died. We looked farther back on the trail and found some bullet craters in the ground with deer hair around them. We also found some twigs that had been broken and trees that had been grazed. We lined up about three of these and concluded that the shooter fired from the top of a nearby hill. On the top of the hill we found five empty .30-caliber shells. We went to the suspect's house, secured his rifle, and later proved via ballistics tests that the shells were fired from his gun. We soon had him before a magistrate. Throughout a deer season we miss violations, but that one didn't get away.

Sure-Shot Pete

Many times like that, deer get wounded and run away and die in the woods. With hunters roaming the woods some of them get reported, but developing a case like the one previous is a long shot. One time a dead deer was reported at the other end of the county, and in the crush of other duties in a hectic season I didn't get to it immediately. The individual that made the report was a noisy kind of person, and was complaining around town about the game warden that wasn't doing his job, and eventually complained again to headquarters.

So, a few days later it was necessary to go explain to him why it appeared I hadn't checked the deer (actually I had, but didn't tell him). He was not at home, but was "out hunting." I managed to find the area and luckily found him hunting with a rifle and a scope sight. He was in a dish-shaped depression about ten yards in diameter. I started to explain to him about the deer as I faced him across the depression. As I spoke, I saw a buck deer come out of the brush behind him just thirty yards or so away. I tried to motion to him with my eyes as the deer started to circle us at the same range. The thought occurred to me to shoot the deer for him with my sidearm; it was certainly close enough, but I quickly dismissed that idea as neither legal nor practical. Finally he got the message, saw the deer, drew up his rifle and aimed. He continued to aim as the deer made a whole half-circle around us, then ran off.

I shouted at him, "Pete, why didn't you shoot?" He replied, "I aimed and all I could see in the scope was fur." When I related this to a couple others who hunted with him, they said, "It probably wouldn't have made a difference. He couldn't have hit it in a vital spot anyway."

Justice Is Served

An officer in our district was having trouble with people placing set lines on the ice of one of the lakes in his area. In Michigan you could use what were called "tipups" for fishing, but these had to be "under immediate control." Setting them, then going to the nearest bar or home or anywhere, leaving what was essentially a fish trap, was illegal. The officer was well-known, and handling it by himself would relegate him to the function of destroying these traps only to have more set somewhere else with better concealment. Three of us went there in plainclothes and made a show of ice fishing in the vicinity where we could keep the latest batch under observation. We spent at least the major part of a day in this effort and were finally rewarded by the appearance of a man going out and checking the lines late in the day. We went over there and accosted him, telling him that he was guilty of the crime. He objected, saying that he just came out and just set the tipups. To be true, the holes were clear of ice as if it was a fresh set, but of course we knew better because we had checked them previously.

"Okay," one of the officers said, "where did you get the minnows for bait? We watched you come on the ice, and you weren't carrying anything."

"Oh, I had them in a bottle in my pocket so they wouldn't freeze," was the answer.

"Well then, where's the bottle?"

"I threw it over toward shore," was the answer.

I looked over that way. There had been a fresh snow the night before, the shoreline was about 70 yards away, and there wasn't a bottle or mark anywhere on the ice. I went over to check his alibi to disprove it. Well, I did find a broken bottle right at the shoreline, but it had been frozen in the ice for some time. We issued a citation to appear before a magistrate, and upon doing so he pleaded "not guilty."

The trial was set for a couple of weeks hence, and in the interim we found that the culprit was not working, living on welfare, and had been for some time, claiming an injury that wouldn't allow him to work. However, it didn't stop him from being a frequent bar occupant where he was spending the welfare money on--well, food? For this practice he was well-known in the community. The county prosecutor took a strong interest in the case and even added additional charges, while the magistrate was reluctant to go along with the case. However, proceed it did, with a jury trial, and after a morning of court process the jury came up with a finding of guilty. The judge, still reluctant, sentenced him to one day in jail whereupon the defendant said, "Hey sheriff, we're just in time for lunch, aren't we?"

We were more than a bit dismayed, as were the prosecutor AND THE JURY. Justice for all the hard work and expense of many? Not even close. But the judge was defeated in the next election just a couple of months later. Justice? You might say so.

Checking winter fishermen on the ice wasn't always difficult. Usually in Michigan the ice freezes, snow falls, the weight of the snow pushes the ice down, and water comes up through cracks and mixes with the snow and makes a mushy ice, which hardens into an irregular surface. Occasionally, the ice hardens enough to resist the pressure, and the ice is clear. Then it gets spooky because it's like walking on a sheet of glass; you can see bottom and you're just never sure how thick that sheet is you're walking on. On a group patrol one of our officers de-cided to bring ice skates, which on those conditions would be effective, especially since it was a large lake. It *was* effective! That day we made several arrests, zooming down on unsuspecting violators. Who woulda thought those SOBs would be skating? The final indignity came as we skated circles around them as we went to shore to the judge.

Harassment?

One time on a nice pleasant calm day I was checking fishermen and some water skiers were zooming around nearby. I got several complaints from the fishermen about "those damn skiers," but from what I could see when I arrived on the scene, they were within their legal limits. I thought I might head off the complaints by bringing it up at the next boat I checked, so I asked if the skiers were bothering them. One fisherman leaned back and smiled and said, "Oh, I don't mind, their wake gives the bait a little action." Those were the kind of encounters that lifted your day.

Enforcing the law puts you in an obvious possibly unfriendly situation with those you contact, but much depends on the officer's demeanor throughout the encounter. Our instructor in recruit school, who was probably no more than 150 pounds in weight, said that he was afraid of no one except a drunk. He explained that he could always reason with anyone except someone whose judgment was addled by alcohol. One night a recruit officer and I were watching for deer shiners and a car approached the field we were in, shining a light around in an apparent attempt to locate deer. The recruit officer ran behind the car, overtook it, and apprehended a man with a loaded gun in the car. After we had arraigned him before a magistrate he thanked us, which gave me one of the surprises of my life.

"The Big Lake"

Being a creature who has always been attracted to water, I was fortunate to be assigned to a county, a peninsula bounded on two sides by Lake Michigan. Recently I visited my old friend Lake Michigan, and I was reminded of her true nature. I'm no stranger to my friend. I've lived alongside her for parts of fifty years, waded in her, swam in her when she wasn't a cold witch, and boated over 200 miles of her surface. But it was always "the big lake," and taken for granted as intimate friends often are. She was just there, embraced by a usually lovely shoreline, but her character--to me at least--was hidden, not obvious, and if she would have shown her character I probably wouldn't have noticed anyway.

My revelation probably could be applied to Huron, Erie, and Ontario as well. Superior is a being of its own, even more mysterious and certainly more dangerous than the others. But of the other lakes I cannot speak. They aren't familiar to me--Michigan is. I've been with her, walked on her beaches, and talked to her--and she's talked to me, but always shyly, covertly, disguising her true nature. My revelation came after living near the ocean for ten years, then returning for a visit to Lake Michigan. For the first time I had something to compare to "the big lake," which caused her character to stand out.

My friend, Lake Michigan, sorry to say, is an unruly spoiled child. She changes her mood quickly: one minute calm and tranquil, the next engaging in a temper tantrum, yet later off on another tack, slapping, snarling, rebellious. The ocean, on the other hand, is mature, an old aunt who's predictable and sedate. True, the ocean can raise her ire and become a destructive demon, but she's slow to anger and gives plenty of warning before doing so. Her angry spells build until immense power pushes over all opposition, but she does so with calculation and forethought, without quickly changing her mood.

Lake Michigan slaps, kicks, and snarls, but then changes her mood like a spoiled little girl, and either runs off somewhere else or pouts. She too has power, but it's a quick-tempered snit rather than a calculated decision. After a tempest she might lie down and purr like a kitten, or even take a quick nap, leaving surfers and sailors becalmed and annoyed. Then as quick as she fell asleep she's ranting off in another direction.

Lake Michigan truly is an inland sea, capable of the same degree of destruction as the salty sea, but her character is entirely different. The stranger to her may think she's an easy conquest because she's so young. Young maybe, but neither innocent nor demure.

I've known that she can be changeable and tempestuous. But now that I've seen her through the same eyes but with a benchmark to judge her, I think I know her a little better. She's an untamed vixen, not just the little girl next door.

It was one of those days that she was resting that my supervisor and I made a sixty-mile run along her shore looking for illegal fishing nets. It was remarkably calm, nothing like the ten-to-twelve- foot waves of which she is capable. This day the entire run was over a glass-like sur-face. This is possible on a partial basis. Changeable as she is, she might be glass-like in one area and stormy in another, but not today. We were investigating mostly submerged logs, soft drink cans, and even took a couple of double takes on floating gull feathers that at a distance looked very suspicious. As mirror-like as the water was, it was almost eerie, distance and perspective being distorted to a great extent.

While on the subject of Lake Michigan, it brings to mind some of my most pleasurable experiences. We were near Grand Traverse Bay of "the big lake." To understand the geography of Grand Traverse Bay, visualize a two-fingered hand seven miles across at the wrist, eleven miles at the knuckles, and one mile at the tips of the fingers, the whole hand being thirty miles long with many protuberances (knuckles or warts) along the way. On a very cold, still winter night it was a distinct pleasure to sit along the shore and listen to it make ice. It was an inharmonious concert, but a magnificent concert nevertheless. There would be huge booms that reverberated in the stillness, crackles that started nearby and ran off in one or more directions; a concert that never ended for long. Sit for a couple hours of Tschaikowsky? I could easily do it for our bay.

This phenomenon is not unique to Lake Michigan, to be sure. Any place where the ice is compressed by the land it could happen, but on our huge embayment that often froze completely it was a beautiful wonder to the ears.

Surrogate Biologist

While most of us were not graduate biologists, we were called on in many instances to play the role the best we could. We often had to autopsy dead deer to look for bullet holes, or if we were lucky, the bullet itself. During one year in my area we had a large die-off of ducks and shorebirds. This, like everything else, happened at unexpected times. We might get a complaint of anything from a dead swan to a mere gull. Mortality in the wild is to be expected, but as similar reports pile in it becomes apparent that normalcy has gone awry and our biologists become concerned. During one year I spent considerable time answering complaints, locating the dead bird or birds, picking them up, and rushing them to professional biologists for analysis before they became too decayed.

Surprise, Surprise

On another occasion I received a complaint of dead trout in a stream in our town of about 500 inhabitants. A new sewer pipe was being put in under the stream, and it was dammed up until they finished, which wouldn't be more than a couple of days. In the press of other priorities I put it low on my to-do list. My reasoning was that the stream was only about two inches deep and maybe eighteen inches wide and two blocks long, it was in town, it didn't even qualify to have a name--after all, how big a problem was it, really? Well, complaints continued to come in, so I reluctantly went to check it out. Yes, I found stranded brook trout, mostly quite small, but some almost seven inches--over 60 of them! Here in a very populated area, in a stream that no one could classify as wild. These I collected and hastily transported to safer water. If there were that many trout in this little stream, how many were there in a wild stream?

Headed in the Same Direction?

We were all in the same department, but while we cooperated with one another, there was a bit of friction between conservation officers, game biologists, foresters, fire officers, and fish biologists. This occurs in many organizations, and the friction might be anywhere from mild joking to serious in-fighting. It's unfortunate that so much effort is spent in activities that just waste resources, and overall cause stress among the "troops." People in those organizations forget that the enemy or the objective is outside, not within.

Other divisions of the department had work to do throughout the state; they didn't just sit in an office and play expert. However, it was disconcerting, to say the least, when a member of the public has a complaint about fish being netted or some such activity to do with the environment, they approach you with it, and you have to proclaim ignorance of the whole affair. It doesn't put the officer in a good light; after all s/he is "the Department" in that area, and not to know what's going on tends to limit either his credibility or capability. Furthermore, it begins to look to the public that the Department isn't very capable either.

Our department was often guilty of this lapse, but it depended on where you were stationed. I heard of one place where a forester was called on the carpet by his supervisor because he merely talked to a fish biologist. Our location was quite good. We realized that we'd gain more by helping one another than by fighting, but there was a little reluctance sometimes and certainly some joshing. We conservation officers often referred to game biologists as "turd counters" because of their procedure of estimating the number of deer in an area by carefully counting the number of droppings in carefully prescribed randomly picked plots in a larger area. When we needed assistance during the busy seasons, fire officers were most likely to help, but others chipped in as well. When the game biologists needed help in game surveys, we were there to help them, and in turn they helped us on occasion in law enforcement. One time I was helping a biologist by the name of Tom. We were embarking from a road into a dense swamp to locate a census location. I knew how dense the cover was where we were heading, and when in the field I usually skirted the bad areas or kept to the contour of hills, but still ending up generally where I wanted to go. But not Tom. He took off on a compass bearing through whatever was in his way. We scrambled through brush, we waded in water, and held true to the bearing. After that I had more respect for biologists than to call them turd counters.

My Wards, the Animals

Considering biology and animals, many people think that conservation officers, being the guardians of such things, were like St. Francis--that we even talked to the animals. That isn't true...not exactly. I *did* talk to some of them on occasion, but they never answered and usually ran away.

Notwithstanding all that, we were called many times to assist with an animal situation that, again, people thought we should be able to handle. This type of situation in most areas today is handled by local government animal control officers, but "in the old days" there was no such entity, so we caught the ball -- and sometimes fumbled it or threw it away.

One notable situation was in about 1961 or so. Two or three homeowners called me when their homes were literally being eaten up by porcupines. Truly it was no concern of mine; porcupines were not protected animals. However, I was curious, and it was also a way I could help someone in distress. What was happening was that the porcupines found a feast on homes faced with plywood in a board-and-batten style. There was something in the plywood that to them was appetizing, so from the ground they would eat up one layer of ply as far as they could reach, then start on the next layer. There was little I could do except furnish the homeowner a live trap to try to catch the cussed critters. But then how do you bait a live trap for an animal with weird tastes like that? I suggested shooting them whenever they were a nuisance, but that was also a problem. They were feeding at night <u>on the house</u>, so did you dare blast them <u>and the house</u> with a shotgun? One man waited up for them several nights and managed to get one or two, but then other porkies even started on the tires and fan belt of his Jeep. Retribution?

On patrol one day I noticed a porkie in a tree next to the house of one of the complainants, so I went over there and shot at him (her?) with my pistol. One shot, two shots, and no movement. I was on the pistol team, so I wasn't a bad shot -- but nothing happened. So I got out my 30-06 rifle and blasted him. Then I remembered the power of such a weapon. Pieces of porcupine, branches, and twigs came raining down on me. A surprise, but problem solved.

The answer to the problem was that the glue that was used to bind the plies together and the salt that clung to the tires and other edible parts of a car were gourmet delights to the porkies. I reported all this in detail to my supervisors; it eventually got to the editor of a national outdoor magazine, and the whole problem was cured when the plywood manu-facturer changed the formula of the glue.

Skunk complaints were also a big issue in my area, and these I had to handle -- skunks were protected furbearers at that time. Skunks are prodigious diggers, and helpful because they eat a lot of insects, but unfortunately they also enjoy the comfort of the ground under hu-man habitations. They can dig a den under a foundation in only a few hours. I can attest to that from my own place when a grand-daddy skunk dug around about 75% of the foundation of my 24 x 40 pole barn. They really aren't bad neighbors when not disturbed, but how do you know you aren't going to disturb them walking around in the dark at the same time that they're out foraging for food? On a very dark night patrol I saw what I thought was a paper blowing by in the wind. I almost kicked at it; good I didn't, because it was a skunk. And family cats? Curiosity is said to kill the cat, and it often gets them a face full of skunk musk when they investigate the wrong hole. If the hole happens to be under a house? BIG trouble!

The usual procedure to be safe was to place a leg-hold trap in their hole, anchored with a chain ten or more feet long. Obviously the trap had to be checked daily, usually in the morning, and if you were suc-cessful you cut a small hole in the bottom of a cardboard box, inserted the end of the chain through the hole, then very carefully, slowly, and patiently pulled the skunk into the box, closed the box, and sprung the trap. They don't enjoy their own scent any more than we do, and a concentrated shot inside the box would not be pleasing to them. You could then transport Mr. Skunk, sore foot and all, far far away, and hopefully he would learn a lesson about messing with humans.

One time I was called to an old-type resort hotel, built around 1900, with a crawl space underneath. A cat had encountered a den of skunks there and the owner had immediately lost all his guests, a really serious situation. I set up in the usual manner, caught a skunk the first night, took him/her away, then set up for another catch. One of the kitchen workers who was from an unnamed major city in New York State watched me make that first catch. Being a curious and helpful person, he apparently wanted to do the next one himself, so without calling me, he tried. Unfortunately, not being familiar with wild things, he didn't realize "carefully, slowly, and patiently," so the hotel got a second dose of skunk odor. If he hadn't been a gourmet cook, my guess is that the owner might have given him a one-way ticket back to Brooklyn.

Intelligence Sources

One officer could not possibly cover his area at all times. It was neces-sary to promote and develop informational sources around the county. Some came to you; others you had to reach out to. This is essential in all police and political work. A simple conservation officer had to be no less proficient in this aspect than the most embedded CIA agent. The level of importance of the information developed was at a different level to be sure, but the methods were the same. After finding sources, which was a delicate procedure where trust was a big factor, the most difficult challenge was the evaluation of incomplete or dubious infor-mation. Was the information fresh? I had recurring reports of serious violations, but in evaluating them I found that they had occurred years before, and the acts had become part of the folklore of the area. Was the report complete enough to be actionable? Some information was just plain incomplete. Sometimes the informant withheld details to protect himself, and who could blame him? Often there just wasn't sufficient data to proceed. What was the motivation of the informant? Was he a true-blue believer, or was he speaking to divert my efforts? I once came upon a man fishing without a license. He said he debated getting one, but one of my chief informers who was also a license agent told him not to bother because the game warden wasn't very sharp. I explained to the fisherman that this time at least the officer was on the case, the case was his, and he got a summons to court. As an aside, I suggested to him that he talk to the license agent about reimbursing him for the fine and costs. Maybe my cooperator was trying to bolster my arrest record, but I doubted him after that.

So overall, intelligence sources varied in credibility. But there was one source that was always true and could always be depended upon: a betrayed wife. That you could count on.

Relations with the Public

Being in uniform, an officer stands out. That obviously is the reason for the uniform. While it can impress the ego, it also carries great responsibility. The uniformed officer in the field is a representative of his unit--and even beyond that, of government as a whole. He or she is expected by the public to be an expert in his field even though he might have to look up the answer, either at the time or later in private. S/he needs to be on good terms with local media and other government officials, even though differences of opinion might exist between them. This contact of course extends to school officials. Much of the officer's time is spent in education, either in or out of the schools, but mostly in. Besides the usual curiosity about game wardens that students held, there was much that could be said about the environment that would fit in with school subjects. In addition to that, we had a state-sponsored hunter safety program that was required of first-time hunters, and we performed as instructors as well as recruiting others to help.

I was often called on to interact with officials much higher "in the food chain" than myself. At one time there was a sportsmen's conference within my district that attracted some very high officials, including the governor and our senator. All of my supervisors were present at the conference and the keynote speaker, a former governor of another state and a former official in Washington, was arriving at the airport near me. I was given the task of getting the speaker from the airport to the conference, a distance of about 50 miles. I recognized that I was in a rarefied atmosphere for one at my position, so was somewhat nervous. Upon arriving, we two headed for the most urgent location after a trip like that: the restroom. Our governor and senator saw us arrive and followed us into the room. I ended up in the embarrassing position of introducing the guest speaker to them while standing facing the wall in front of a porcelain fixture. If I had any feelings that I was in with "the big boys," it vanished immediately because of my embarrassment.

Interesting Dilemma

On a day off I was fishing with a friend and we passed by a boat with three fishermen in it. On a whim, I decided to check them. They had no valid licenses, but they did have short-term licenses which had expired about a month previously. Michigan had a program of selling these short-term licenses, which would last two weeks as a convenience for vacationers who didn't need an annual license. I was taken aback with the situation because the cost of the annual license was little more than the short-term license. I remarked that I should give them "tickets," but didn't feel that was appropriate. One of them mentioned, "Yes, that would be embarrassing," but he didn't elaborate. I found out where they were staying and gave them until the next day to buy annual licenses. When I went back the next day I found that I had apprehended the mayor, chief of police, and chief of detectives of a city in a nearby state. It was to their credit that they hadn't tried to exert their influence the day before. We got several laughs over the affair, even to the point of my being photographed simulating handcuffing the chief of police.

Who Would Have Known?

At another time, another officer and I were assigned to give a presentation to a conference of nuns. We were to speak to them about educating young people about the environment, biology "light," and fish and game laws. I had brought along with me most of my reference manuals and books plus some handouts. Following our presentation we invited them to look over our materials and take some handouts. Well! They lost the definition between handouts and references and almost cleaned me out. Gotta look out for those nuns!

Patrol Partners

For the most part, an officer would patrol his own area alone in his own vehicle. It would be wasteful to have two-man (or -woman) patrols when little was going on. On some days, irrespective of some instances recounted above, it was almost wasteful to have even one officer patrolling. Some days just <u>nothing</u> was happening. Weather had much to do with that, but even on nice days it was often quiet. It almost seemed as if some sort of cycle was affecting nature. In counterpoint to the slack times, it seemed sometimes as if all nature was going crazy. Deer would run in front of cars, not to mention smaller animals which would be killed, people would do dumb things for which they could or would be arrested, and it would all occur in a span of a couple of days. Then events would cool off again for a while. It was during the "hot" periods when one officer was taxed to keep up, and a patrol partner was helpful. Few enterprises, including the government, can afford to have people standing around for several days waiting for something to happen. Usually during these busy periods someone from the officer's own department--a forest fire officer, or others would be available. Sometimes we patrolled accompanied by a sheriff's deputy, or even a civilian who was interested, but then there were potential problems with liability concerns. Day patrols were no problem for the most part, but night patrols were not only dangerous alone, but also non-productive. One officer just couldn't maintain the necessary control when it was dark. I found that our family pet, a German Shepherd, was a low-cost asset, was very helpful in the job, and in some respects could do it better than I.

When we got her as a pet she was a puppy, ready for training. I gave her an unusual name for a German Shepherd, "Susie," just to counter the ferocious names usually given to such a dog. Whatever name she might have been given, she was efficient, perhaps even better than a human might have been. Humans can be bluffed, but a dog – not often. One cannot say enough for a *smart* dog, well-trained, in the law enforcement field. The emphasis is on "well-trained" because a scantily trained dog would not only be a hindrance but a liability.

Susie helped me on many occasions when I would come upon a group, usually hunters, when one officer can keep his eyes on only so much. Occasionally I would get the question, "Does that dog bite?" My answer was, "Only if provoked, but don't ever run from her; she's a chaser." That kept the group in one place where I could deal with them one by one without any defections. Four specific instances of her aid are noteworthy.

As mentioned, in those days we picked up highway-killed deer, and there were many to pick up. Most often, since the deer move at night, that's when they would be crossing a road and be hit. Usually someone who called in that they had hit a deer wasn't very sure where <u>they</u> were or where the deer had gone for certain since it was dark. So, to make the search as quickly as possible, Susie went with me on these trips. Upon arriving in the general area all I had to do was say, "Susie, where's the deer?" and she would find it.

One morning I got a call of a dead deer halfway across the county. I went to the informant's house, and it took me about 45 minutes to get there. He told me it was about a mile away, and he would show me the spot. He joined me, and we went to pick it up. He pointed it out to me, about 60 yards from where we parked. I told him, "I see it, but let the dog find it. It's part of her training." So I said the magic words: "Susie, where's the deer?" and she began tracking off down the highway shoulder. When she arrived at the spot she reached out for a nose-to-nose encounter, then quickly jumped back. I thought that was strange, because she had never done that before. When we got there and picked up the deer it started to kick. It was still alive, but mortally wounded so that it couldn't get up. It had to have been lying there for at least an hour, probably longer.

Another day, which was a day off for me well before the legal deer season, I received a call from a tavern. You don't just announce, "Sorry, I can't come, it's my day off," especially to a bunch of guys in a bar. That would be negative advertising at its worst. I was told that someone had shot a deer right across the road from the tavern and had gone into the woods to pursue it. Susie and I loaded into the car and hurried to the spot. After arriving, all I had to do was utter the magic words, "Susie, where's the deer?" She proceeded to put her nose to the ground and track her way into the woods. She kept veering to the left and I kept correcting her to the right, following the directions I had gotten from the informant. She reluctantly followed me, but as we proceeded it became obvious it was the wrong way. We back-tracked to where I had steered her and she again headed off to the left. Reluctantly bowing to superior knowledge I followed her, and it wasn't long before she found a blood trail. Okay, dumb me. It wasn't a lot of blood, perhaps more than I could have tracked myself, but she had better equipment with which to work. Eventually we lost the trail, hopefully because the deer waited for the blood to clot, then took off somewhat safe but injured. Meanwhile Susie was probably mumbling about that dumb boss of hers.

On another occasion I was really proud of her. It was another day off for me, and I was at home and got a call from the state police that a trooper had a probable case to be investigated. It was a few days before the duck season and he was driving along the highway adjacent to a bay where the water was very shallow and there were small ponds. He heard a shot, looked over, saw a duck fall, and saw two men, one with a shotgun or rifle. He turned his car around, stopped, and spoke to them. "What? Duck? No, we don't know anything about that," was the answer.

So I was called. Susie and I jumped in the car, and went to the location. The trooper turned it over to me. I searched along the shoreline and found the shotgun hidden behind a tree. Even with this revelation they denied anything to do with a duck. Although it was very suspect, at this point I had nothing. It was legal to have a gun out in that area. So I tried a bluff. I got Susie out of the car and asked her, "Susie, where's the duck?" Now, she knew deer, but she didn't know a duck from an elm tree, yet she dashed off across the rocks and reeds and doggone if she didn't find it, still barely alive. Then upon returning to shore I started writing out a couple of tickets. I'm sure word got out about that among the populace. She was gaining a better reputation than I had.

On another occasion there had been a drowning on a small lake in my area, and the sheriff's people were already there, plus a few spectators. I was in the area, so I went there to see if I could be helpful. Upon arrival I got out of the car and let Susie out also. One of the spectators said, "Oh, is that the dog I've been hearing about?" I answered in the affirmative. He said, "What does she do?" I called her over, and said, "Susie, where's the deer?" His car was parked about 20 yards away. She immediately went over and sniffed at the trunk lid of his car. All startled, he said, "Uh-oh, maybe I better let you look in there." I told him I had no evidence to direct me there except Susie, but if he wanted to let me look, I would. I did, but of course there wasn't anything there. There probably *had* been not too far in the past if Susie was right, and she wasn't wrong very often. But it was another feather in her cap for people to talk about. Her performance on this occasion was outstanding, as it often was, and I could have hugged her on the spot if I was sure other stories wouldn't be going round the county about the "weird" conservation officer.

Fooled

I cannot speak for other conservation officers, but I have to believe that I was fooled on many occasions. What's lost to many in the public is that a law enforcement officer has to make split-second decisions with less than complete information. Sometimes his life may be at stake, sometimes it's a matter of releasing people in his custody, sometimes a matter of losing critical information on a case. Under our legal system an officer has to err in the favor of a suspect, and that's as it should be. I can admit to at least four times when I came out with egg on my face.

Shots Fired?

Early in my career I went to bed one night and was almost asleep. My being still groggy might account for my action. I heard shots not far from town. I jumped into my clothes, got in the car, and charged out into the countryside. It was not at all busy; I found no one roaming around, and very few cars. I finally realized it was the 4th of July, and what I concluded were shots were more than likely firecrackers. Oh well; back to bed.

With Friends Like These ----

Another time early in my career my wife and I were invited to dinner by a couple in a nearby town. I was flattered and happy that perhaps we could make some new friends. We went there and found that two other couples were there. Well! Even better: a chance to meet even more people. So we dined and talked, then it was time to depart. No, they wouldn't have any of that. I should go over with them to visit this or that, and the evening stretched longer and longer. It wasn't until weeks later that I heard veiled assertions that I had been duped while other friends of our dinner partners were out shining deer.

Who's the Dullard?

Late in a deer season, just about dusk, my partner and I came upon a rather nondescript car parked along the road near a large swampy area. Two young men were standing alongside it with a deer on the trunk. We stopped and checked them. They were exuberant over their buck, which was a nice six point and was properly tagged, except that it was obviously not a fresh kill. The eyes were sunken into the head and if it had been a warmer day it might even have smelled. However, the boys were very happy about it. They seemed in my judgment to be a few cards less than a full deck, it was the last day of the season, and it <u>was</u> a nice rack of horns, so I let it go. It was months later that I realized that I probably should have checked <u>in the trunk</u> for an illegal deer. So, who was the dumb one?

Look Out Downriver!

On one fine day another officer and I decided to make a canoe patrol of a popular fishing river. We launched the canoe and proceeded downstream. Fishing was light, but we did check a few fishermen. Rounding a bend we came upon a fisherman wading in the center of the river, working a hole just downstream. We debated whether to check him, and decided in the affirmative. We approached, and I, in the bow, asked him for his license. While holding his fishing pole in one hand he began digging in his pocket with the other. Meanwhile, my partner ceased backwatering with his paddle, the current caught us, and we ended up broadside to the current against the fisherman who was being pushed downstream into the hole by our canoe. He was gritting his teeth as he tried to keep his footing against the current and us, hold on to his fishing pole, and dig in his pocket for his license. I wouldn't have blamed him if he capsized us, and I certainly wouldn't pull a bonehead stunt like that again.

Balloon Baloney

In another deer season we came upon a group of hunters, a car, and a dead deer. One of the hunters was walking out of a swamp with blood on his hands. One told of a weather balloon caught in a tree in a woods about two miles away, and they all chimed in on that theme. I suspected that they had another deer back in the swamp, but where? The weather balloon story was on the verge of unbelievable, but I played along with it, intending to go to a nearby bluff where we could watch their actions more intensely. We did so, but by the time we got up on the bluff they had departed. We did kind of keep our eyes peeled for weather balloons in trees, but never took it seriously. Also, we didn't see their car again either.

A True Tree Story

The deer season in Michigan, as in many other states, occurs in November, which in that area is one of the most unpredictable months for weather. Many ships have gone down in the Great Lakes during November gales, most notably the *Carl Bradley* and the *Francisco Morazan*, which didn't actually go down but ended up piling into South Manitou Island in Lake Michigan. The deer season therefore can include anything from "blue bird" weather to a blizzard, and many hunters decked out in heavy clothes often end up shedding them. One evening my partner and I were patrolling an area when those "white mosquitos" started falling from the sky. It was still relatively warm, somewhere in the zone where snow is most slippery.

We were traveling along a paved road which I knew reasonably well and the snow had built up to about an inch or so. As I came to a slight rise I knew there was a curve ahead after topping the hill. I wasn't traveling very fast therefore, maybe 30 to 35. However, I had forgotten how abrupt the curve was. As I topped the hill I began easing the speed with judicious use of the brakes, but saw that making the curve was going to be dicey because we were sliding whenever I touched the brake pedal and the crown of the road was sending us toward the shoulder. On the right was a guard rail protecting a slight dropoff and close to the right of that a row of maple trees. I found us about to straddle the guard rail, and that not being a good option, I steered between the guard rail and the trees. My partner riding in the jump seat was a forester. I finally got us stopped between the trees and the rail, but the car leaned into one of the trees, slightly stoving in the back passenger's side door. My partner, his eyes wide open, said, "I was looking right down the fender at the biggest maple tree I ever saw in my life!"

All in All ----

So, we tried to keep the environment from being despoiled and also tried to make sure all who wanted to participate got a fair share of nature's bounty. We were and are a small force against anyone who wants to get the other guy's share as well as his own. We missed a lot; we were fooled a lot. But along the way we met some mean people and some good ones. The good ones far outnumbered the bad ones. The bad ones usually got a chance to reconsider their actions after they paid fines, stood jail time, or whatever the judge wanted to mete out. Whether they wanted to change or not, they always had to face the fact that penalties "next time" were likely to be more severe.

www.ingramcontent.com/pod-product-compliance
Lightning Source LLC
Chambersburg PA
CBHW060003300526
45794CB00003B/1069